sick
JOKES

G. ROOSOM

summersdale

REALLY SICK JOKES

Summersdale Publishers Ltd
46 West Street
Chichester
West Sussex
PO19 1RP
UK

www.summersdale.com

Printed and bound in Great Britain

ISBN: 1-84024-538-7

ISBN: 978-1-84024-538-7

REALLY

sick

JOKES

What's green
one minute and
red the next?

A frog in a blender.

REALLY
sick
JOKES

Dave goes into the Gents and
finds a man with no arms
standing next to the urinal.
Wondering to himself how the
man copes, he takes a piss
and is about to leave when
the man asks if he wouldn't
mind helping him out. Feeling
charitable, Dave agrees to
give him a hand. He unzips the
man's jeans to reveal his lurid
green, foul-smelling penis.
'Poor guy,' thinks Dave.
'Some people have no luck.'

6

Holding his breath, Dave helps the guy finish his business and zips his flies up for him. 'Thanks,' the man says. 'Not many people would do a thing like that for a stranger.' 'That's no problem,' replies Dave, 'but what's wrong with your penis?' Pulling his arms out of his jacket, he shrugs and says, 'No idea, but I didn't want to touch it.'

How do you know
when you've mixed up
the oral thermometer
and the rectal
thermometer?

They taste different.

A man with a huge abscess on his arm decided to watch a film to take his mind off the pain. Some time after he sat down in the cinema, the man on his right looked at him and threw up. Outraged, the first man said, 'I know I look disgusting, but there's no need for that!' 'It's not you,' the man apologised; 'I just realised I've been dipping my nachos in your abscess instead of my cheese.'

9

Two hungry tramps are walking the streets at night and come across a dead dog. One of them starts devouring it immediately. After a while he notices the second tramp hasn't touched it and says, 'You must be starving too – we can share it.' 'No way,' replies the second tramp. 'That dog's cold and disgusting! Who knows how long it's been there.' The first tramp happily continues, until there is nothing left but bones. Later, he starts to feel sick and regurgitates the dog remains. The second tramp rubs his hands together and says, 'That's what I've been waiting for. I haven't had a hot meal in days!'

What's the difference between a young man and an old man?

An old man has wet farts and dry dreams.

A boy vampire sent a girl vampire a bright red heart for Valentine's Day. 'Did you get the heart I sent you?' he asked. 'Oh yes, thank you, it was lovely,' she replied. 'And it was still beating.'

A man was driving in the
countryside late one night
when his car broke down. He
was miles from anywhere and
decided to walk back to the
last farmhouse he had seen.
He explained his predicament
to the farmer and asked if he
could stay there the night. They
had no spare rooms, but the
farmer said, 'If you promise not
to lay a finger on my daughter,
you can sleep in her bed.'
The man agreed and went

straight to bed. In the morning
he asked the farmer how
much he owed for the room.
'Nothing at all, since you had
to share,' replied the farmer.
'Thanks,' said the man. 'And
don't worry — your daughter
was so cold I didn't go near her.'
'I'm not surprised,' said
the farmer. 'We're burying
her tomorrow.'

How do you know
a blonde's having
a bad day?

She's got a tampon
behind her ear and she
can't find her pencil.

Little Tommy was out shopping
with his mum and said,
'Mum, I really need a piss.'
'It's very rude to say "piss",
Tommy. Next time, just say
you have to whisper instead,'
she told him. Later that week,
Tommy's father was driving
him to school when Tommy
announced, 'Dad, I really need
to whisper.' 'OK son,' his dad
said. 'Just whisper in my ear.'

Howard goes into a restaurant
and orders a chicken curry.
'We've run out, I'm afraid. He
ordered the last bowl,' says
the waitress, pointing to the
man next to him. The man
has obviously had enough, as
he's sitting back smoking a
cigarette, but the bowl is still
full. 'Are you going to eat that?'
says Howard. 'No, be my guest,'
replies the man, pushing the
bowl towards him. Howard tucks
in, but after a few mouthfuls he

sees a cockroach in the curry and vomits back into the bowl. The other bloke turns to him and says, 'That's exactly what happened to me, mate.'

What do you call an
elf with his head up
a fairy's dress?

A goblin.

Patient: Doctor, doctor, there's something wrong with me — everything I eat comes out exactly the same the other end. If I eat carrots, carrots come out, and if I eat chocolate éclairs, chocolate éclairs come out. What should I do?
Doctor: Hmm… Why don't you try eating shit?

Three men are lost in the desert when they come upon a cave. Hoping that there might be some food or water inside, the first man volunteers to investigate. Sure enough, sitting on a slab of stone in the centre of the cave is a peanut butter sandwich. But just as he reaches out to take a bite, a terrifying voice booms out, 'Do not touch that sandwich...' He flees in fright and tells the others there is a haunted sandwich in the cave. The second man decides to brave it, enters the cave and is about to take a bite when the voice booms out again. He flees. The third man, who is starving by this stage, strides into the cave, picks up the sandwich and takes a huge bite. As he's chewing, the voice booms, 'I told you once. I told you twice. I wiped my arse between the slice.'

What's sicker than
eating chocolate
drops off the floor?

Finding out they're
not chocolate drops.

A man ties up his dog outside a country pub, kisses its bum, then enters the pub and orders a pint. The bartender gives him his drink and can't resist asking him why he kissed the dog's bum. 'My lips are chapped,' replied the man. 'Is that some kind of natural remedy?' asked the bartender. 'No, but it stops me wanting to lick them.'

A dead man arrives in hell
and is being shown around by
Beelzebub. 'There are three
ways you can spend the rest
of eternity,' Beelzebub informs
him. 'The choice is yours.'
First, he shows the man a room
where the men and women are
being continually flayed with
barbed whips. In the second
room, the man sees people
being forced to skin each
other with potato peelers. In
the third room, everyone is

standing knee deep in a putrid mix of vomit, faeces and fish guts, but apart from that they seem to be having a good time, chatting and enjoying tea and biscuits. 'I think I'll spend eternity here,' says the man, entering the room. 'All right everyone,' says Beelzebub. 'Break's over. Back on your heads.'

What happened
when the lepers
played poker?

One of them threw
in their hand and the
rest started laughing
their heads off.

Stuck in traffic, a cabby decided to share some tales with his passenger to pass the time. He told him about his visit to a factory in South America, where the workers made latex gloves by dipping a hand into boiling hot liquid latex and putting it into cold water to set the glove. Seeing the horrified look on the passenger's face, the cabby added, 'You probably don't want to know how they make condoms then.'

Brian pops round to his parents' after work one day, but finds they're not home. He lets himself in with the spare key. He decides to have a snack while he waits for them to arrive and finds a dish of leftover spaghetti Bolognese. He heats it up, adds some salt and pepper and tucks in. His parents walk through the door and stare, appalled, at the dish in front of him. 'Oh sorry,' he said. 'I couldn't resist the

leftover spaghetti Bolognese.'
'That's not spaghetti
Bolognese!' his father shouts.
'That's the dog's faeces sample
we were going to take to the
vet's. He's got worms.'

What did the blind
man say as he passed
a fish market?

'Hello ladies!'

A man phones his boss one morning and says, 'I'm afraid I can't make it to work today. I'm sick.' 'Oh dear — have you caught this nasty bug that's going round?' asks his boss. 'Oh no, I feel fine,' says the man. 'But I've got my willy stuck up the vacuum cleaner.' 'You're right,' says his boss, 'you are sick.'

A young blonde woman went to see her doctor. She was so gorgeous that he lost all self-control and told her to undress for a full examination, saying it was now standard NHS procedure with new patients. He began by caressing her buttocks, 'Can you tell me what I'm doing?' he asked. 'You're examining me for skin irritations,' she replied. 'Correct,' said the doctor as he started to massage her breasts. 'And can you tell me what I'm doing now?'

34

'You're examining my breasts for lumps,' she replied. 'That's right,' said the old pervert. He couldn't believe his luck and was very excited. He climbed onto the examining bed and started having sex with her. 'Now can you tell me what I'm doing?' he asked her. 'You're getting what you deserve,' she replied. 'I've got gonorrhoea.'

What has four legs
and one hand?

A happy Rottweiler.

A vicar approached the organist one sunday to discuss hymns before a service. On top of the organ he noticed a bowl of water with a condom floating in it. Baffled by this display he asked the organist to explain. 'Well vicar,' she said, 'I found it on the bus and the instructions said it would prevent disease if you put it on your organ and kept it moist. It really must be working as I've never felt better.'

Two doctors were discussing a new nurse's progress. 'I have noticed that Nikki does everything the wrong way round,' one doctor complained. 'She's crazy!' the second doctor replied. 'Yesterday she nearly killed a man giving him 90 milligrams of morphine every 30 minutes, instead of 30 milligrams every 90 minutes!' A deafening scream interrupted their conversation. 'Oh no!' shouted the first doctor.

'I just remembered I told Nurse Nikki to prick Mr Johnson's boil!'

What do you get if
you lie under a cow?

A pat on the head.

Two old men were out for a stroll in the park when they saw a dog licking its balls. One old man said to the other, 'Cor, I wish I could do that!' The other man answered, 'It's probably best to stroke him first.'

A little boy went into the supermarket and bought a box of washing powder. The checkout assistant said, 'That's very good of you, to help your mum with the laundry.' 'I'm not doing any laundry,' he said. 'This is to wash my dog.' 'I don't think that would be very good for your dog: he might get ill,' the assistant replied. 'Why don't you try something else?' No matter what the assistant said, she

42

could not talk the boy out of
buying the washing powder.
A week later the boy was back
at the shop buying sweets. The
assistant was eager to find
out what happened with the
dog and the washing powder.
'I'm afraid he died,' the little
boy said. 'But before you
say it, it wasn't the washing
powder that killed him. I think
it was the tumble dryer.'

What do you call a man with no arms and legs who lies on your doorstep?

Matt.

One day, two sisters were walking through the fields when they came across some sheep droppings. 'What are those?' asked the younger sister. 'They're clever pills,' the older sister told her. 'If you eat them, they make you clever.' 'Eurgh! They taste of poo!' exclaimed the little sister, after chewing a couple. 'I told you,' the older sister said. 'You're clever already.'

A cannibal took his son out
for his first hunting lesson.
They found a good spot next
to a forest path and the father
said, 'Now we just wait for
something to turn up and
we'll take it home for dinner.'
'There's one, Dad,' the
son said as an old lady
hobbled down the path.
'Oh no, son, that's too
small to feed the family.'
'How about that one, Dad? He's
big enough,' the son said as

a fat man walked into view.
'Oh no, son, that'll be too fatty.'
Later in the afternoon a
beautiful woman appeared.
'That one's perfect, Dad.
We can definitely eat her,'
the son said gleefully.
'Oh no, not her!' the father said.
'Why not, Dad?' the son
asked, a little confused.
'Because we're going to keep
her and eat your mother!'

Who's more sick, a supermarket owner or a supermarket owner's son?

The son: he's a little grocer.

A man was sitting at the bar, complaining of constipation. 'I've tried everything – even prune juice didn't work.' 'Have you tried these?' the bartender suggested, handing him a packet of laxatives. 'Guaranteed to work by 9 a.m.' The man gratefully took the laxatives and went home. The next day he came storming into the pub. 'Didn't they work?' asked the bartender. 'Oh, they worked fine,' he fumed, 'only I didn't wake up till midday!'

A woman was invited to dinner at her in-laws for the first time. She knew her husband was fairly messy and so expected the same of his parents. At the dinner table she noticed that the plates were filthy and couldn't help but ask, 'Are these plates even clean?' 'Soap and water couldn't get them any cleaner,' the mother-in-law replied. They finished dinner, and despite the grimy plate, the woman quite enjoyed it and said so.

'I'm glad, dear,' said her mother-in-law, getting up to clear the table. Having collected the plates she opened the back door and called, 'Here Soap, here Water! Din dins!'

What did the
mathematician do when
he was constipated?

He worked it out with
a pen and paper.

A lady is trapped with her baby on the tenth floor of a tower block as a fire rages below. She is screaming and doesn't know what to do when out of the crowd steps the star of the local rugby team. 'Throw me your baby,' he calls up to the terrified woman. 'I will catch it.' The woman throws him her baby, which he catches… and then proceeds to drop kick over a nearby fence.

A teenaged girl was going on
a hot date wearing a chiffon
top, but no bra. 'You can't go
out like that!' her grandmother
shrieked. The girl shrugged
indifferently as she left, saying,
'Chill out. These days it's OK
to flash your fairy lights.' Later,
when the girl returned with
her date, she was mortified to
find her grandmother sitting by
the fire with her wrinkly chest
exposed. 'Chill out, darling,'
her grandmother said. 'If it's

54

OK for you to twinkle your
fairy lights, I think I can show
off my Chinese lanterns.'

What's sicker than
farting in the bath?

Following through.

A girl and a boy are snogging behind the bike sheds at break time. They finally come up for air and the girl says, 'You're an amazing kisser, but I'd rather you weren't chewing gum.' 'I'm not chewing gum,' the boy replied. 'I've got bronchitis.'

Three men on a desert island were captured by natives. The king told them they would be killed, unless they could pass a test. First, they must find three of the same fruit and return to the king. The first man came back with plums. The king told him; 'To complete the test you must squeeze all the fruit up your bum, but if you make any noise, you will be killed.' On the second plum he let out a quiet groan, and the tribe promptly killed him. The second man returned with grapes, heard the next part of the test and was certain he would pass. But on the third grape he started laughing hysterically and his throat was slit. Surprised to see him up in heaven, the first guy asked, 'What happened? You nearly passed the test.' 'Well,' said the second man, 'I saw the other guy coming back with coconuts!'

Why did the leper
always drive at
the speed limit?

He couldn't take
his eyes off the
speedometer.

A notorious street gang leader always wore a red shirt. One day, a gang member called Biff asked him why. 'Because I might get shot, and I don't want you all to freak out at the sight of blood,' he answered. A little later the gang were walking down the street when a rival gang approached, all wielding weapons. Biff glanced over at his leader and said, 'Looks like you should have worn your brown pants too.'

A couple from London were visiting the woman's family in Surrey, and the man soon began to tire of the countryside. 'Why don't you take the dogs into the woods and have a go at shooting?' his father-in-law suggested. Off he went with the dogs in tow, glad that he finally had something to do. A few hours later he came back to the house looking more cheerful than he had all week. 'That was brilliant fun,'

he said to his father-in-law,
handing him back the gun. 'Do
you have any more dogs?'

Why does eating
oysters improve
your sex life?

Because after
eating that, you'll
eat anything.

Two vomits are in a bar
drowning their sorrows. They
eventually leave at closing
time and one of them starts
to smile as they approach a
kebab shop on the corner.
'You've changed your tune,'
the other says. 'What's
cheered you up so quickly?'
'This place brings back
happy memories. It's where
I was brought up!'

On his first day as a door-to-door mouthwash salesman, a man only sold one bottle. He knew this wasn't good enough so the next day he went to a better area to see if he could sell any more, but only managed to sell two. This still wasn't good enough, so he decided he needed a gimmick to increase his sales. The next day he set up a stand giving away free apple juice. A bloke walked over, drank a glass of the apple juice and said, 'This tastes like piss!' The salesman replied, 'That's because it is. Can I tempt you with our new brand of mouthwash?'

What do Captain
Jean-Luc Picard
and toilet paper
have in common?

They both try to rid
Uranus of Klingons.

A man selling electric carpet cleaners walks straight into a woman's house and throws a bag of manure onto her carpet. Absolutely livid, the woman screams abuse at him. 'Calm down,' he reassures her. 'I'll eat whatever this machine doesn't clean up.' She goes into her kitchen and returns with a knife and fork. 'You might need these,' she says with a smirk. 'Our electricity got cut off last week.'

Jeff and his son noticed that their cat had become cross-eyed so they took it to the vet. 'That's easily cured,' said the vet, sticking a tube up the cat's bum. He blew sharply down the tube until the cat's eyes were straight again. 'That'll be £100,' the vet told Jeff, and they took the cat home. A few days later, the boy noticed the cat's eyes were crossed again. Not wanting his dad to spend another £100, he decided to

sort the problem out himself.
He stuck a straw up the cat's
bum and blew down it but,
oddly, nothing happened, so he
called his sister over to help.
She took out the tube, turned
it around and started to blow.
'What on earth did you do
that for?' he asked his sister.
'I didn't want to use the end
YOU had in your mouth, did I?!'

A pirate went for a job interview at a theme park. The interviewer asked him if his eye-patch and hook were real. 'They're real: I lost my hand fighting scoundrels at sea.' 'And what about your eye?' 'I lost that when my parrot crapped in it,' the pirate replied. 'I didn't realise that could do so much damage!' the interviewer said. 'Well, it wouldn't have, but it was the first day I got my hook.'

Ann had been working in a
pharmacy for a few weeks,
but was on her final warning
for missing out on sales. She
could never seem to find the
items customers requested.
That morning, a man walked
in with a terrible cough and
asked for something to stop
it. Ann couldn't find the cough
medicine and, afraid her boss
would fire her, sold him a bottle
of laxative and told him to take
it straight away. Ann's boss

was very proud that she had
helped the customer and
asked her what she had sold.
Ann told her boss everything.
'You can't cure a cough with
laxative!' he fumed. 'Actually,
I think it's worked,' Ann said,
pointing outside at the man.
'He's too scared to cough.'

Which serial killer
dispatched his victims
with tinned ham?

The Son of Spam.

A man goes to see his doctor and says, 'I've considered it carefully, and I've decided to have a castration.' The doctor tries to dissuade him, but the man is adamant, and so the doctor books him in for the procedure. He wakes up after surgery, sees a man in the bed opposite and asks what he's in for. 'I just had a circumcision,' he answered. 'How about you?' 'OH MY GOD! That's what I meant!'

A group of first-year medical
students were receiving their
introductory lecture on autopsy.
Standing next to the cadaver,
the professor announced that
there were two essential skills
required in an autopsy. 'The
first,' he said, 'is to overcome
your fear of the body.' As he
said this he inserted his finger
into the corpse's anus. He then
proceeded to lick his finger, and
instructed the students to do
the same. With much grimacing,

the students all followed suit. 'Secondly,' the professor said, 'you must have sharp observation skills. You should have noticed that I inserted my index finger, but licked my middle finger.'

What do you call
a man with a bad
case of catarrh?

Fleming.

An elderly woman accompanies her husband to his regular medical check-up. The nurse at reception asks him for a urine and faeces sample, but the old man can't hear so she repeats, 'I'll need a urine and faeces sample, sir.' The old man still doesn't get it, so his wife turns and shouts across the room, 'She needs to see a pair of your underpants, Harold!'

An old woman goes to her local shop to buy two cans of cat food. The shop assistant refuses to sell her the cat food without first seeing the cat. Later that week, she returns to the shop for two cans of dog food, but again the assistant refuses to sell her the dog food without seeing the dog. She returns a third time holding a cardboard box, goes up to the assistant and asks him to feel inside.

'It's warm and squishy. What is it?' asks the shop assistant. 'Well,' says the old lady, 'maybe now you'll let me buy two rolls of toilet paper.'

What's the difference between bogeys and Brussels sprouts?

You can't get children to eat Brussels sprouts.

A man walked into a Welsh pub and was greeted by silent stares from the locals. 'Not from round here, are you?' said the landlord. 'Where you from, son?' 'I'm from up north,' the man said politely. 'Oh really, and what do you do up north?' the landlord asked. 'I'm a taxidermist,' he told the landlord. 'I stuff animals.' Looking relieved, the landlord shouted to the rest of the pub, 'It's all right! He's one of us!'

A businessman was staying in an exclusive hotel. His stomach was upset due to something he had eaten, and he spent all night going back and forth to the bathroom with false alarms. Eventually, he decided to ignore the warning signs, only this time he soiled the bed with a violent explosion of pungent diarrhoea. In a fit of shame and anxiety, he flung the bed linen out of the hotel window. In the street below, they landed on a hippie walking by. Enveloped in the sheets, the hippie flailed about wildly, until he finally managed to extract himself from the tangled mess. 'Whoa,' he said, staring at the pile of sheets in disbelief. 'I just beat the crap out of a ghost!'

What is soft and warm
when you go to bed,
but hard and stiff
when you wake up?

Vomit.

REALLY
sick
JOKES

A man goes to see his doctor. 'I've got a strawberry stuck up my bum,' he says. 'What can I do?' The doctor replies, 'I can give you some cream for that.'

Three men are lost in the jungle. After walking for two days without eating or drinking, they come across a dead body, which looks like it may have been there for some time. By this stage they are starving, so they decide to tuck in, but first a discussion breaks out over how to divide up the corpse.

'As a dedicated Hearts supporter,' says the first man, 'I suppose I should eat the heart.'

'I support Liverpool, so I

should eat the liver,' says
the second man. The third
man says, 'I support Arsenal,
but I've lost my appetite.'

Why don't elephants
pick their noses?

Have you ever tried to
hide a 20 lb bogey?

A beautiful woman walked up behind a waiter in a restaurant and whispered seductively in his ear, 'Are you the manager?' 'N-No,' he stuttered. 'Maybe you can help me anyway,' she breathed, running her fingers over his lips. 'Of course,' said the waiter. She slid her fingers into his mouth. 'Would you give him a message?' He sucked on her fingers and nodded.

REALLY
sick
JOKES

'Tell him he needs to put
more toilet roll and towels
in the bathroom.'

Two old men are out fishing in extremely cold weather. Reg reels in fish after fish, but Bert doesn't catch so much as a tadpole. Exasperated, Bert finally asks Reg how he catches so many fish. 'Uummmb bmmm mmmm mmm mm,' replies Reg. No idea what Reg is trying to say, Bert asks him again what his trick is. 'Uummmb bmmm mmmm mmm mm,' repeats Reg. 'Sorry, I still don't know what you're saying,' Bert tells him.

Reg then spits something
out and says, 'I've been
keeping my maggots warm.'

What's brown, smelly
and sits steaming on
top of a piano stool?

Mozart's last
movement.

REALLY SICK JOKES

A father is looking after his young daughter while his wife is at work. The girl skips around and says 'Daddy, look!' and wiggles a finger at him. Recognising a game he's seen his wife playing with her, he says, 'Daddy's going to gobble up your finger!' and pretends to eat her finger. The little girl bursts into tears. 'What's wrong, sweetheart,' he says, 'did I play the game wrong?' The little girl wails, 'Daddy, where's my bogey gone?'

A woman goes to a restaurant and orders some fish and chips. As she's running late for a meeting, she rushes her meal and a fish bone gets stuck in her throat. Two local boys at the opposite table see her choking and rush to her aid. The first boy drops his trousers and bends over and the second boy starts licking his bum hole. The woman is so disgusted by this sight she is violently sick, and the bone flies from her throat.

The two boys sit back down at their table and one says to the other, 'That hind-lick manoeuvre works every time.'

How can you tell the
difference between a
turd and a biscuit?

Try dunking them
in your tea.

A man goes into a barbershop and asks for a really close shave. 'No problem,' says the barber, producing a large marble. 'Pop this in your mouth and position it between your cheek and gum.' The man follows his instructions and the barber begins to shave the man's chin with immaculate precision. After a few strokes, the man mumbles indistinctly, 'What if I swallow it?' 'Oh, just bring it back tomorrow as everyone else does.'

Striding through the forest one
day, a rambler comes across
a man lying on the ground.
It doesn't look like the man
is breathing. Panicking, the
rambler dials 999 from his
mobile. 'I found a man in the
woods. I think he's dead!' he
wails. The operator calms him
down and explains what he
needs to do. 'Firstly, you have
to make sure the man is dead.'
The phone line goes quiet
and then the operator hears

a sickening crunch. 'Right,'
the rambler says, returning
to the phone. 'What's next?'

What happened
when the Pope went
to Mount Olive?

Popeye nearly
killed him.

At breakfast time a man is eating a bowl of cornflakes and says to his wife, 'These new cornflakes are really delicious.' 'They're not cornflakes!' she shrieked. 'That's little Billy's scab collection!'

After putting in a carpet for a
customer, the carpet layer went
outside to roll up a cigarette,
but couldn't find his tobacco. He
went back inside to look for it
and discovered a bump under
the carpet. Not wanting to pull
up the entire carpet for a pack
of tobacco, he squashed the
lump with his mallet. Just as
he was leaving, his customer
returned, and admired the
lovely job he'd done with her
carpet. 'I found this in the

kitchen,' she said, holding a pack of tobacco. 'It must be yours. Oh, and I don't' suppose you've seen my hamster?'

How do you know when you've got really bad acne?

A blind man tries to read your face.

A woman has an appointment with her bank manager and is waiting in his office. She notices a dish of peanuts on the desk and can't help but eat a handful. She is waiting quite a while and by the time the bank manager arrives she's eaten them all. She feels terrible and apologises to him. 'That's OK, I don't eat them anyway,' he replies. 'I just suck the chocolate off the M&Ms.'

On a night out with the lads, Billy meets a gorgeous woman and they end up back at her place. 'We'll have to be quiet,' she tells him. 'My parents will kill me if they find you here!' The couple are getting friendly on the couch until Billy pulls away and says, 'I really need to use your bathroom.' 'My parents will hear you if you go upstairs,' she told him. 'You better just use the kitchen sink.' Billy tiptoes off into the kitchen.

A few minutes later he
returns and whispers,
'Have you got any toilet roll?'

What do you call a
teenaged bunny?

A pubic hare.

REALLY
sick
JOKES

A cannibal family are having dinner when the youngest son blurts out, 'I really hate my sister.' 'That's OK son,' his father replies. 'Just leave her on the side of your plate.'

A little boy lived next door
to the fire station and one
day he went to show the
firemen his own little fire
engine. He was wearing a
fireman's costume, and had
a garden hose and little
ladders hung on his red
trailer. The little boy's dog
was pulling the trailer along.
Very impressed by the boy's
fire engine, the firemen went
to have a closer look. They
noticed that the poor dog

was tied on by his balls. 'Wouldn't it be better to tie that onto his collar?' one of them suggested. The little boy replied, 'Well then what would I use as a siren?'

What's sick?

Finding a toenail in
your milkshake.

What's sicker
than sick?

Finding the rest of the
toe in your hotdog.

Two statues, a lady and a
gentleman, had looked out
majestically over the gardens
of Buckingham Palace for over
a century. One day, an angel
popped down from heaven and
said to them, 'You've both done
a sterling job here all these
years. I think I'll give you a little
treat. I will bring you to life for
thirty minutes, which you may
spend doing whatever you like.'
And with that, the two statues
sprang into life, winked at one

another and disappeared off into the topiary. The angel began to blush a little at the amount of giggling and rustling he could hear. After only twenty minutes, the statues reappeared, both beaming from ear to ear. 'Still ten minutes to go,' said the angel, with a raised eyebrow. 'Oh spiffing,' said the lady statue, and with a cheeky grin she turned to the gentleman statue and said, 'Darling, this time you catch the pigeon, and I'll poo in his eye.'

Did you hear about
the butcher who
kept backing into his
mincing machine?

He was always getting
behind in his work.

On the first night of their
holiday, a young couple are
enjoying a romantic walk along
the beach. The girl, desperate
for the toilet, wants to go back
to the hotel. 'Why don't you
just go behind that rock?' her
boyfriend suggests. 'There's
no one around.' Keeping
watch, he gets aroused thinking
of her half undressed and
reaches out to surprise her...
but feels something long and
stiff. 'What the hell! When did

you have your sex changed?'
he screams. 'I didn't,' she
said. 'I needed a shit as well.'

Also Available

REALLY

GROSS

FACTS

EVERYTHING YOU DON'T
NEED TO KNOW BUT CAN'T
RESIST READING ABOUT

TED LEECH

REALLY GROSS FACTS

TED LEECH

£2.99

Paperback

What grosses you out? How about this:

- Attila the Hun died from drowning in his own nosebleed.
- The best recorded distance for projectile vomiting is 8 metres.
- One pound of peanut butter can contain up to 150 bug fragments and five rodent hairs.

This crusty, thoroughly distasteful and utterly compelling book of facts will disgust your friends and give hours of revolting, sickening pleasure.

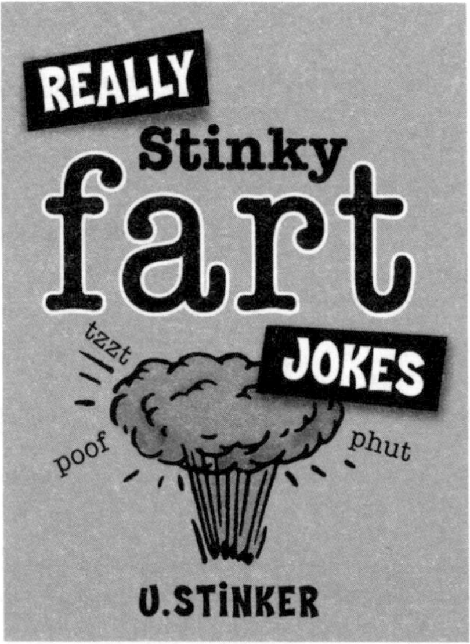
REALLY
Stinky
fart
JOKES
tzzt
poof
phut
U.STINKER

REALLY STINKY FART JOKES

U. STINKER

£2.99

Paperback

'Did you here about the blind skunk?
He's dating a fart.'

There's no denying it – flatulence is funny. Bath bubblers, duvet fluffers and follow-throughs: this pungent little book has a joke for every farting occasion.

One whiff of these little stinkers will have you gagging for more.

www.summersdale.com